First Field Trips

Zoo

by Rebecca Pettiford

Bullfrog Books

Ideas for Parents and Teachers

Bullfrog Books let children practice reading informational text at the earliest reading levels. Repetition, familiar words, and photo labels support early readers.

Before Reading
- Discuss the cover photo. What does it tell them?

- Look at the picture glossary together. Read and discuss the words.

Read the Book
- "Walk" through the book and look at the photos. Let the child ask questions. Point out the photo labels.

- Read the book to the child, or have him or her read independently.

After Reading
- Prompt the child to think more. Ask: Have you been to the zoo? What was your favorite animal to watch?

Bullfrog Books are published by Jump!
5357 Penn Avenue South
Minneapolis, MN 55419
www.jumplibrary.com

Library of Congress Cataloging-in-Publication Data

Pettiford, Rebecca, author.
  Zoo / by Rebecca Pettiford.
  Description: Minneapolis, MN: Jump!, Inc., [2016]
  Series: First field trips
  Audience: Ages 5–8.
  Audience: K to grade 3.
Includes bibliographical references and index.
LCCN 2015038110|
ISBN 9781620312995 (hardcover: alk. paper)
ISBN 9781624963650 (ebook)
Subjects: LCSH: Zoos—Juvenile literature. |
Zoo animals—Juvenile literature. | School field
trips—Juvenile literature.
LCC QL76.P45 2016
DDC 590.73—dc23

Editor: Jenny Fretland VanVoorst
Series Designer: Ellen Huber
Book Designer: Lindaanne Donohoe
Photo Researcher: Lindaanne Donohoe

Photo Credits: All photos by Shutterstock except:
Dreamstime, cover; iStock, 4; SuperStock, 6–7.

Printed in the United States of America at
Corporate Graphics in North Mankato, Minnesota.

Table of Contents

A Day at the Zoo

Our class is on a field trip.

We are at the zoo.

Nick is the zookeeper.
He takes care of
the animals.

Look! It's an elephant!

It is the biggest
land animal.

Nick lets us feed a giraffe.

It is tall.

It has a long neck.

Roar! It's a lion.

It has sharp teeth.

Lions live in Africa.

We go to the
reptile house.

Dan holds a snake.

Kay touches a crocodile.

Its skin is bumpy.

We go to the aviary.
Birds fly and screech.
Nina likes the parrots.

We go to a show.
Seals do tricks.
They get fish.

We had fun at the zoo!

Animals at the Zoo

elephant

parrot

giraffe

lion

Picture Glossary

Africa
The second-largest continent on Earth; it is south of Europe and Asia.

reptile
A cold-blooded animal such as a snake or crocodile.

aviary
A big cage or building in which birds are kept.

zookeeper
A person who takes care of zoo animals.

Index

To Learn More

Learning more is as easy as 1, 2, 3.

1) Go to www.factsurfer.com

2) Enter "zoo" into the search box.

3) Click the "Surf" button to see a list of websites.

With factsurfer.com, finding more information is just a click away.